Movie Animals

BY CONNIE COLWELL MILLER

amicus
high interest

Amicus High Interest is an imprint of Amicus
P.O. Box 1329, Mankato, MN 56002
www.amicuspublishing.us

Library of Congress Cataloging-in-Publication Data
Miller, Connie Colwell, 1976-
 Movie animals / by Connie Colwell Miller.
    pages cm. -- (Animals with jobs)
 Includes index.
 Summary: "Describes animals that might work in movies,
how they are trained, and what a day is like on a movie set.
Includes information about movie animals in history and
what it's like to train animals to work in a movie"--Provided by
publisher.
 ISBN 978-1-60753-379-5 (library binding) -- ISBN 978-1-
60753-427-3 (ebook)
1. Animals in motion pictures--Juvenile literature. I. Title.
 PN1995.9.A5M55 2014
 791.43'662--dc23
                                    2013001421

Editor   Wendy Dieker
Series Designer   Kathleen Petelinsek
Page production   Red Line Editorial, Inc.

Photo Credits
Pictorial Press LTD/Alamy, cover; Shutterstock Images,
4, 8, 20; Mikel Martinez/Shutterstock Images, 7; Getty
Images, 11; AF Archive/Alamy, 12; Xavier Marchant/
Shutterstock Images, 15; JP Chretien/Shutterstock Images,
16; iStockphoto/Thinkstock, 19; Sonya Etchison/Shutterstock
Images, 23; Shawn Zhang/Shutterstock Images, 24;
Featureflash/Shutterstock Images, 27; Stu Porter/Shutterstock
Images, 28

Printed in the United States at Corporate Graphics in North
Mankato, Minnesota.
4-2013/1151
10 9 8 7 6 5 4 3 2 1

Table of Contents

This dog plays with a soccer ball, just like Chip does in the movie.

4

A Day on Set

A mutt named Chip has just come to the movie set. Chip is a movie star. He is in a film called *Soccer Dog*. It's time for Chip to get to work!

Chip's trainer is Roger. Roger shows Chip what to do. Today, he needs to walk up a ramp to a door. He needs to open the door and go inside. Then he has to let the door slam behind him.

The film starts rolling. Roger tells Chip
what to do from off-screen. Chip starts up
the ramp. But he goes up too quickly. He
tries again. This time, the door won't shut
behind him. But the third time is perfect!
The man behind the camera stops filming.
The director is happy. "Nice work, Chip!"

Chip probably learned how to go
up and down ramps like this dog.

Elephants can be in movies, too!

 Where do trainers find their animals?

What kinds of animals can work in show biz? Any kind that can be trained. Many are dogs like Chip. But they can be bears, tigers, or wolves. They could be dolphins, orcas, horses, or cats. Chimps and orangutans have starred in movies. Even mice and birds have been movie stars.

 It depends. Dogs are often found at rescue shelters. Other animals are bred for training. These could be bears, wolves, or tigers.

Famous Animal Movie Stars

Lassie is a very famous movie star. A collie named Pal played this smart dog in a movie. It was called *Lassie Come Home*. Later, Pal's son played Lassie in a TV series. Over the years, many of Pal's other **offspring** played Lassie, too.

10

Buddy played football in the movie *Golden Receiver.*

The 1997 movie *Air Bud* starred a golden retriever. His name was Buddy. In this film, Buddy has a special talent. He can play basketball. In 1998, Buddy starred in another movie. This one was called *Air Bud: Golden Receiver*. Buddy played football in this film! Buddy did many of the tricks. But he didn't do them all. Some tricks were made with special effects.

In 1993, *Free Willy* starred an orca named Keiko. Since he was two, Keiko had lived in **captivity**. In the movie, Keiko swam with a boy in a large pool. The boy touched Keiko's nose. He rubbed Keiko's tongue. Keiko and the boy did these tricks for the camera. The money made by the movie helped Keiko. His trainers used it to get Keiko ready to return to the ocean.

 How do you train an orca?

Keiko looked like this orca. Orcas are also called killer whales.

 Just like you train other animals. Orcas are given treats, like fish. But trainers don't speak commands. They blow a high-pitched whistle.

Horses get rewarded with treats when they do a good job.

Learning the Job

Movie animals work hard. They spend hundreds of hours practicing with their trainers. Some learn to obey their trainers' words. Other animals respond to sounds like whistles. But all animals do their jobs in order to get tasty treats. After training, the animals do their work on camera.

Most of the time, the animals work for food treats. A mouse might be trained to scurry across a floor. She runs to reach a treat of nuts and cheese. But the nuts and cheese are off-screen. Movie viewers will only see the scurrying mouse.

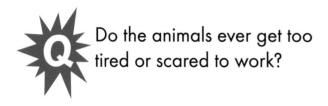 Do the animals ever get too tired or scared to work?

Mice love nuts. They will run across the floor to get them.

 Yes. Sometimes, more than one animal plays a role. If one animal gets tired, it can rest. Another animal that looks like it can fill in.

Trainers must love animals. Dolphin trainers must also love to swim.

Becoming a Partner

Would you like to train movie animals? You have to love working with animals. Trainers might live with their animals. That means they take care of them day and night. Some animals start training very young. Animal trainers should be ready for a lot of hard work.

Sometimes animal stars are in a movie with people. A dog might have to pretend to be a boy's pet. The boy learns how to work with the dog. The dog and boy also have to get to know each other. They spend a lot of time together. Then they will be good friends when the filming finally starts.

Animal stars and their actor partners become good friends.

Trainers must be careful with their animals. They must not work them too much or too hard. Animals can't talk. That means trainers must watch them carefully. They look for signs of **exhaustion**. Specially trained workers watch animals on movie sets. They make sure none are treated badly. They make sure they don't work too hard.

This orangutan takes a rest.

Animal Stars

Animal stars come in all shapes and sizes. In the past, dogs were the most common movie animals. That's because they are easiest to train. But **exotic** animals can be movie stars, too. Movies like *We Bought a Zoo* and *Zookeeper* starred lions and tigers and bears. Oh, my!

These actors worked with lions in the movie *To Walk with Lions*.

Animators will use CGI to copy this one zebra and make a herd.

Q What are some movies that have used CGI for animals?

Today, some movies don't use live animals. Instead, they use **computer-generated imaging (CGI)**. One script calls for a herd of zebras running on the plains. A filmmaker films one zebra running. Then, computer workers copy that image. Now it looks like dozens of zebras running.

Animals have starred in many movies. They add plenty of humor and fun.

 The guinea pigs in *G-Force* were done with CGI. But the penguins in *Mr. Popper's Penguins* were real. CGI was used for some scenes, though.

Glossary

captivity Cared for by humans in a cage or aquarium; an animal in captivity is not in its natural habitat.

computer-generated imaging (CGI) Using computer graphics to create special effects.

exhaustion Extreme tiredness.

exotic Unusual.

offspring Children or young.

Read More

Goldish, Meish. *Hollywood Horses.* Horse Power. Bearport Publishing, 2008.

Hutmacher, Kimberly Marie. *Television and Movie Star Dogs.* Pebble Plus: Working Dogs. Capstone Press, 2011.

Presnall, Judith Janda. *Animal Actors.* Animals with Jobs. KidHaven Press, 2001.

Websites

American Humane Association: Pawscars
http://www.americanhumane.org/about-us/newsroom/news-releases/and-the-pawscar-goes-to.html

Animal Planet
http://animal.discovery.com/

Animal Trainer for Film and Television
http://www.netplaces.com/working-with-animals/jobs-in-entertainment/animal-trainer-for-film-and-television.htm

Index

About the Author

Connie Colwell Miller is a writer, editor, and teacher of writing. She has written over 70 books for young readers. She especially enjoys writing about animals because she is one. She lives in Mankato, Minnesota, with her husband and three children.